HOME LIFE DURING THE AMERICAN REVOLUTION

by Emma Carlson-Berne

CAPSTONE PRESS
a capstone imprint

Published by Capstone Press, an imprint of Capstone
1710 Roe Crest Drive, North Mankato, Minnesota 56003
capstonepub.com

Library of Congress Cataloging-in-Publication Data is available on the Library of Congress website.
ISBN: 9798875254406 (hardcover)
ISBN: 9798875254352 (paperback)
ISBN: 9798875254369 (ebook PDF)

Summary: Narrative text looks the American Revolution and how it affected people's home lives.

Editorial Credits: Editor: Mandy Robbins; Designer: Elijah Blue; Media Researcher: Rebekah Hubstenberger; Production Specialist: Tori Abraham

Image Credits
Alamy: Alex Garland, 22, Archivad, 12, ART Collection, 27, Lebrecht Music & Arts, 7, Science History Images, 13; Associated Press: North Wind Picture Archives, 21; Getty Images: benoitb, 15, Hulton Archive, 5, iStock/Christine_Kohler, 23, iStock/KenWiedemann, 17, Kean Collection, 11, 14, powerofforever, cover (top); Granger: 24, Sarin Images, 9; Library of Congress: Prints & Photographs Division, cover (bottom), 19; Shutterstock: chrupka, 25, IgorGolovniov, 28, kintore (globe icon), cover, 1, nik_nadal (magnifying glass), cover, 1, Robert Plociennik (texture background), cover and throughout, Yuliia_Pizhivska (star border), cover and throughout

Printed and bound in China. 006459

TABLE OF CONTENTS

Words in **BOLD** are in the glossary.

Chapter 1

CHOOSING A SIDE

The American Revolutionary War began in 1775. Colonists prepared for a war in their own backyards. Fighting took place in cornfields, orchards, and pastures. Messengers and spies rode between houses and **taverns**. Everyone's lives were affected. It didn't matter if they were white, Black, or Native people, free or **enslaved**, man, woman, or child.

Not all colonists were on the same side during the war. Neighbors sometimes took opposing sides. About one-third to one-half of the colonists were patriots. They wanted independence from Great Britain. Another one-fifth to one-third were loyalists. They supported King George III and the British government. And the remaining people were **neutral**. The war affected people differently depending on who they were, where they lived, and what their views were on the war.

American fighters face British forces at the Battle of Lexington and Concord.

Some loyalists joined up with the British Army. Enslaved Black men had the most motivation to join. The British promised them freedom.

But even loyalists who didn't fight found ways to support King George and the British government. Some worked as spies for the British. Others wrote **pamphlets** or published essays speaking out against the patriots.

Many loyalists faced violence for their views. People who supported the British government were sometimes tarred and feathered or beaten. Their homes and property were burned by patriot supporters. Some decided to leave the colonies once war broke out and return to Great Britain. Others stayed but kept their views quiet.

FACT!

Myles Cooper and Charles Inglis were loyalist ministers. They wrote pamphlets against the revolution and in support of the British government.

Patriot leaders try to stop an angry mob from attacking loyalists inside a building.

At the start of the war, many loyalists believed the British troops only needed to win one battle to defeat the Americans. But that's not what happened. By the end of the war, about 60,000 loyalists left the colonies. They returned to England or **immigrated** to other English colonies.

The American Revolution at a Glance

What?

The American Revolution (also called the Revolutionary War)

When?

1775–1783

Where?

New Hampshire, Massachusetts, Rhode Island, Connecticut, New York, New Jersey, Pennsylvania, Delaware, Maryland, Virginia, North Carolina, South Carolina, and Georgia.

Why?

- Discontent about taxes from the British government
- Lack of representation in Parliament
- Punishments the British placed on the colonists

Many loyalists felt pressure to leave the United States after the revolution.

Chapter 2

WOMEN DURING THE WAR

The Revolutionary War changed the lives of almost every woman in the colonies. Husbands, brothers, and sons left to fight in the battles. Many women were left behind. They ran farms, shops, and households. Some women struggled to support their families.

Of white colonists, wives and daughters of lower-level workers had it the hardest. Many left their homes and traveled to cities to look for work.

When battles came close to their homes, many women nursed wounded soldiers. They offered food and clothing to soldiers, even if they were strangers.

Women often organized with friends and neighbors. Together, they sewed uniforms and made bullets. Other women's clubs raised money for the military cause they supported.

An American woman protects her home from British soldiers.

Women and children follow along with marching soldiers.

Other women followed the army camps to keep their families together. Children came too. In camp, they cooked, did laundry, and nursed the men. Some women used their skills to make money. Soldiers could pay to have their uniforms repaired, clothes washed, or a hot meal cooked.

FACT!

Women working in army camps were supposed to be paid in meat and bread. They were expected to follow the same orders and routines as the soldiers.

Both sides also used women as spies. Women could enter camps or the edges of battles without raising suspicion. Lydia Darragh was a Quaker woman who spied for the Continental Army. When British officers used her home for meetings, Lydia convinced them to let her stay. She listened to their conversations. She passed on notes in code to her son, a soldier in the Continental Army.

Lydia Darragh passes information to a Continental soldier.

Women in Battle

Women were not supposed to fight in battles, but they were there. When help was needed, women worked on cannon crews. They brought water for the soldiers to drink and to cool down the cannons after they were fired. After battles, women nursed wounded soldiers.

A patriot woman stokes a cannon in battle.

Women's powers sometimes came through their pens. Phyllis Wheatley was an enslaved person. She became the first Black person from the United States to publish a book. Wheatley was a poet in her 20s during the Revolutionary War. She wrote about liberty and **morality**. She became well-known and was respected by George Washington himself. Her enslavers eventually released her.

Phyllis Wheatley

Deborah Sampson, Soldier

Deborah Sampson was a woman from Massachusetts who wanted to fight in the Revolutionary War. She dressed as a man and enlisted in the Continental Army as Robert Shirtliff. She served as a soldier, and differing stories tell of her fighting and being wounded in battle. It's hard to know what the exact true story of her service was, but her secret was eventually uncovered. She was honorably discharged.

Chapter 3

HOW THE WAR AFFECTED CHILDREN

Colonial children from all backgrounds were affected a during the war, too. Many children were left at home on farms or in shops. They took over the roles of older brothers and fathers. In army camps, they helped their mothers or grandmothers cook and do laundry.

Children and teenagers made good spies too. They could walk into camps and along roads without being suspected. One story tells of a 16-year-old girl named Sybil Ludington. She learned that the British were planning to attack the Continental Army in April 1777. According to legend, she rode her horse 40 miles (64 kilometers) to warn Continental troops. As with many women and children of that time, no official record exists of her brave act.

"Tory" was another word for loyalist.

On the Battlefield

Army camps became home for many children. They trailed along with their families. At the age of 16, boys could be soldiers. But before 16, they still could work as army messengers, drummers, and **fife** players. They could also load cannons, bring water to cool them afterward, and serve officers. All these jobs brought boys onto the battlefield along with the soldiers.

Some boys lied about their age so they could enlist sooner. As many as two percent of the Continental Army was made up of soldiers younger than 16. Most of these boys were between the ages of 13 and 15.

FACT!

Connecticut boy Samuel Aspenwall joined the army at age 15, in 1782.

Chapter 4

NATIVE PEOPLE CAUGHT IN THE MIDDLE

The lives of Native people were upended during the American Revolution as well. About 250,000 Native people belonging to about 80 tribes lived east of the Mississippi River. Many tribes tried to stay neutral when fighting broke out. They did not want to harm trading relationships or bring violence to their communities.

As fighting continued, Native groups ended up taking sides. Many tribes were concerned with the expansion of settlers onto Native lands. Before the war, the British government had tried to keep European settlers away from Native lands. Colonists had wanted to settle and expand.

Many Native groups fought for the British. They had trading relationships and military friendships with the British government. They trusted the British more than the colonists to help protect their land.

Other groups sided with the colonists. These people had trading relationships and alliances with colonists that they wanted to preserve.

The Stockbridge Community

A mixed group of Mohican, Housatonic, and Wappinger Indians lived among the colonists in the town of Stockbridge, Massachusetts. The community sent 17 warriors to fight for the patriots during the **Siege** of Boston in 1775.

Throughout the war, the Stockbridge Indians lost 40 of their warriors. But the patriots did not help them. The Stockbridge community had a hard time supporting itself with the loss of these members.

The Continental government had promised land to the men who fought. The government did not give that land to the widows of the men who had died. Worse yet, when the Stockbridge Indians asked the Continental Congress to protect land they already had, Congress refused to help.

Conditions in Valley Forge were brutal during the winter of 1777 to 1778.

Polly Cooper

Polly Cooper was an Oneida woman. She brought food and clothing to the starving, freezing Continental soldiers at Valley Forge, during the winter of 1777 to 1778. She gave them corn that her people had harvested and showed them how to cook it.

Split Nations

The war caused division within some Native groups. The Iroquois Confederacy was a large group of six nations. Each nation was made up of many tribes, and they couldn't agree on which side to take. The Mohawk, Seneca, Cayuga, and Onondaga nations sided with the British. The Oneida and Tuscarora fought with the patriots. These nations had previously agreed to be allies. The Revolutionary War threw them into conflict with each other.

American soldiers burn down an Iroquois village.

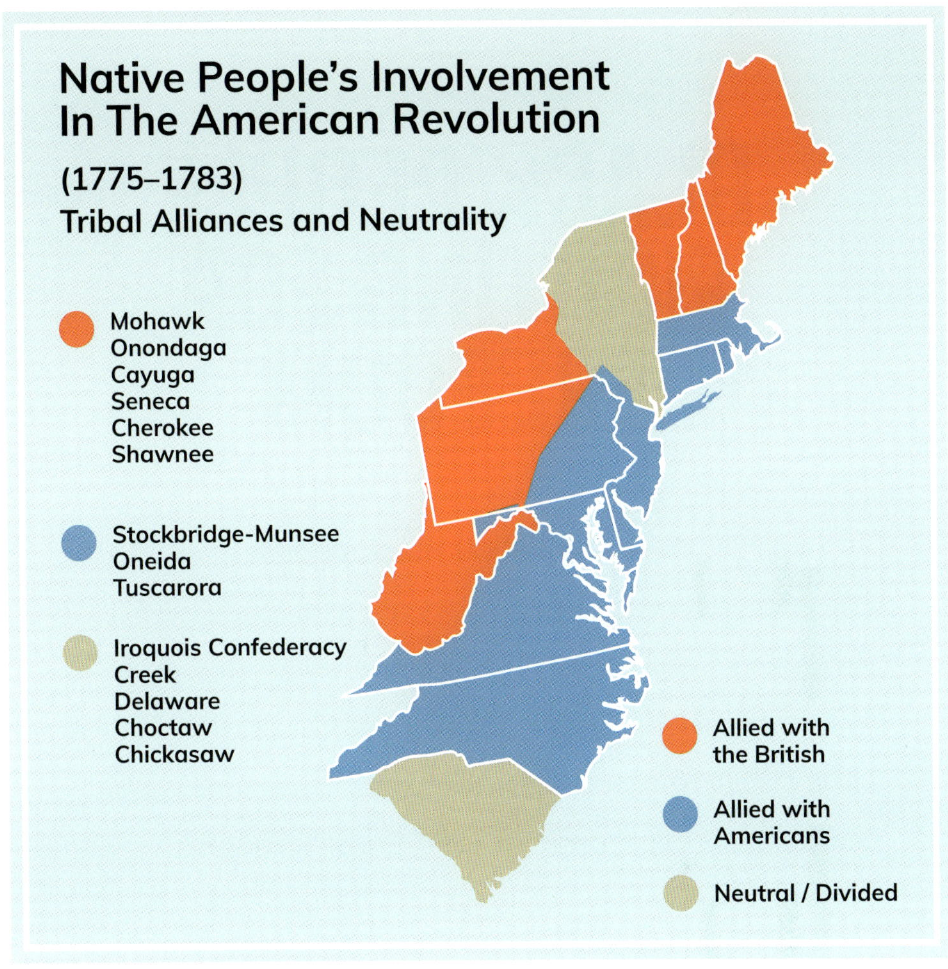

Just as colonial towns and homes were burned or destroyed, Native villages were also devastated in the war. When Native groups fighting for the British attacked Continental soldiers, the army would ransack their villages. In 1777, George Washington ordered one of his generals to burn Iroquois villages and crops in a widespread act of destruction.

Chapter 5

BLACK PEOPLE FIGHTING FOR FREEDOM

In 1776, around 500,000 Black people lived in the colonies. About 90 percent were enslaved. The British promised freedom to enslaved men who fled and joined the British army. Others fought on the patriot side, either in place of or alongside their enslavers. Some states eventually offered them freedom.

At home, enslaved people took on more tasks as men went to war. Some spied for one side or the other. Since enslaved people worked in houses, shops, and farms, they often heard news to pass along.

One story tells of an enslaved person named Quaco. He was said to have worked in the kitchen of a loyalist officer. Quaco listened to conversations. He took note of a British general's movements and passed the information to the patriots.

Harry Washington

Harry Washington was enslaved at Mount Vernon, George Washington's large farm in Virginia. In 1775, Virginia's loyalist governor offered freedom to enslaved men who fled patriot enslavers to be soldiers for the British. Harry Washington joined the crew of a British warship. After the war, Harry moved to Nova Scotia and then to Sierra Leone in Africa.

Enslaved people worked long, hard days on plantations.

Salem Poor

Salem Poor was born enslaved but purchased his own freedom in 1769. Poor enlisted in a Massachusetts branch of the Continental Army in 1775 and fought at the Battle of Bunker Hill. Poor and other Black soldiers in the unit were supposed to merely dig **fortifications**. But they found themselves fighting the British with muskets and rifles after retreating patriot soldiers had run out of ammunition.

In 1775, a U.S. stamp was released honoring Salem Poor.

Revolutionary War Timeline

April 1775	The first battles at Lexington and Concord occur.
May 1775	The Continental Congress votes to form the Continental Army with Washington as its leader.
June 1775	The Battle of Bunker Hill is won by the British, who suffer heavy casualties.
March 1776	The Continental Army pushes the British out of Boston.
July 1776	The Continental Congress votes to adopt the Declaration of Independence.
Sept. 1776	New York falls under British control.
Dec. 1776	The Continental Army captures Trenton after crossing the Delaware River.
Sept.-Oct. 1777	The Americans win the Battle of Saratoga.
Dec. 1777	The Continental Army begins a long, cold encampment at Valley Forge in Pennsylvania.
Feb. 1778	France enters the war as an American ally against the British.
Oct. 1781	The British army loses the Battle of Yorktown and surrenders to the Continental Army. The United States wins the war.
Sept. 3, 1783	The Revolutionary War is officially over with the signing of the Treaty of Paris.

Glossary

enslaved (en-SLAYVD)—to be treated as property and forced to work for no pay

fife (FYFE)—a small musical instrument similar to a flute

fortification (for-tuh-fih-KAY-shun)—a building or wall built as a military defense

immigrate (IM-uh-grate)—to come from one country to live permanently in another country

morality (moh-RA-luh-tee)—beliefs about what is right and wrong behavior

neutral (NOO-truhl)—not taking any side in war

pamphlet (PAM-fluht)—a small booklet

siege (SEEJ)—a military blockade of a city, to make it surrender

tavern (TA-vurn)—a place where people can buy and drink alcoholic beverages; taverns were popular gathering places in the 1700s

Read More

Gagne, Tammy. *Fact and Fiction of the American Revolution*. Minneapolis: ABDO Publishing Company, 2022.

Murray, Hallie. *The Role of Women in the American Revolution*. New York: Cavendish Square, 2020.

Silva, Sadie. *The American Revolution*. Berkeley Heights, NJ: Enslow Publishers, 2023.

Internet Sites

The American Revolution
kids.britannica.com/kids/article/American-Revolution/353711

Answers to Questions Kids Ask About the Revolutionary War
battlefields.org/learn/articles/answers-questions-kids-ask-about-revolutionary-war

History for Kids: The American Revolution
historyforkids.org/american-revolution-facts-information-for-kids/

Index

About the Author

Emma Carlson Berne has written many books for young readers. She lives in Cincinnati, Ohio, with her husband, three boys, one grumpy cat, and one friendly cat.